How does a piano make music?

Disney BOOKS BY MAIL

DK Direct Limited
Managing Art Editor Eljay Crompton
Senior Editor Rosemary McCormick
Writer Alexandra Parsons
Illustrators The Alvin White Studios and Richard Manning
Designers Wayne Blades, Veneta Bullen, Richard Clemson,
Sarah Goodwin, Diane Klein, Sonia Whillock

Photograph on page 26 Courtesy of
London Features International

Contents

What is music?

It is an arrangement of sounds that is pleasing to our ears and to our minds. Music can make us feel happy or sad. This power gives music a special magic and makes it popular all over the world. Ancient peoples thought that music was a gift from the gods.

La la la and boom chica boom!

☞ Music is made up of three things: melody, which is the tune; harmony, which is notes sounded together; and rhythm, that's the beat!

Making waves

Sounds are made by air shivering and shaking. Sounds travel through the air in invisible waves. Each sound makes a different shape of wave.

Blow that horn

What tuba can't you play?

A tuba toothpaste!

What was the first musical instrument?

The human voice! Some people, of course, are better singers than others, but everyone can try. The human voice makes sound when breath is pushed past the vocal cords, making them shake. That shaking is called vibrating and, as we all know, sounds are heard when air vibrates!

A

B

Play those cords!

Your vocal cords are in a special place in your throat called the larynx. When you are silent, the cords are loose and relaxed like the rubber bands in diagram A. But when you speak, they tighten up like the rubber bands in diagram B.

Can you hear me at the back?
Trained singers can make their voices heard at the back of a concert hall – even over the sound of a full orchestra.

Do re mi facts

A scale is a set of eight notes arranged in steps going up and coming down again. Singers practice by singing scales. Each step has been given a name. All together now – Do, Re, Mi, Fa, Sol, La, Ti, Do.

How many different kinds of music are there?

There is something for everyone! There are slow, sad songs like the blues; rhythmic songs like reggae and rap; songs that tell stories; and music without words. In China, some music is made with gongs and bells. African songs are full of rhythm. And Spanish music often has the lively sound of castanets.

Computer games
People who make up new tunes are called composers. Modern composers sometimes use computers to create new music.

A special sound
Music from India also has its own special sound. The sitar is a very popular instrument in India.

9

Tuneful facts

☞ Sailors used to sing work songs called sea shanties. The rhythmic songs made everyone pull together.

☞ Church hymns were probably the first European songs heard in America.

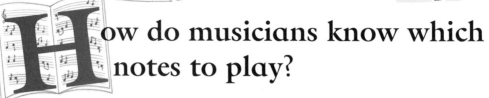

How do musicians know which notes to play?

Many musicians can read music, and some play by "ear." Musical notes are written down on special paper printed with sets of five lines. These lines are called a staff. Notes are written as dots on the lines and in the spaces, so musicians know which notes to play or sing.

Take it from the top!

This is what written-down music looks like. Just as the words in a book make sense to people who can read, these lines and dots make sense to people who have learned to read music.

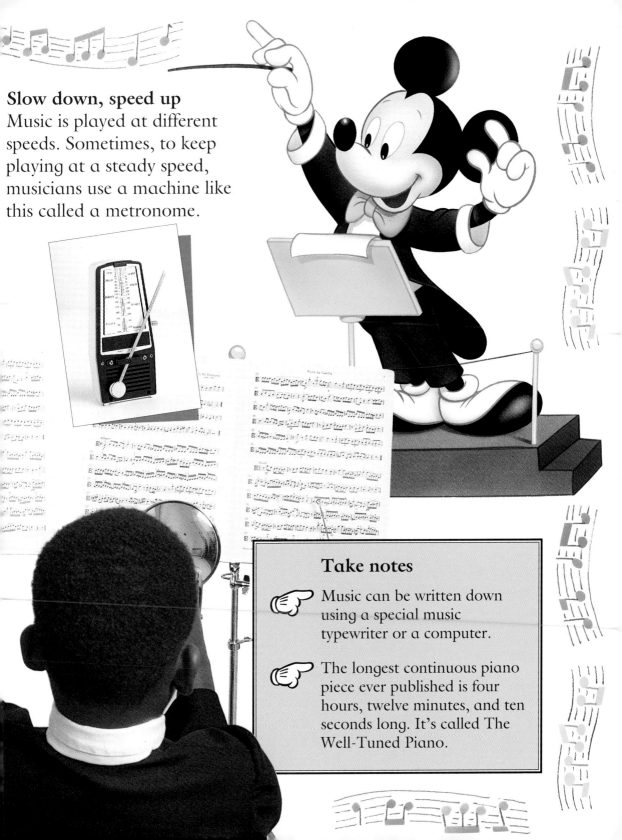

Slow down, speed up

Music is played at different speeds. Sometimes, to keep playing at a steady speed, musicians use a machine like this called a metronome.

Take notes

☞ Music can be written down using a special music typewriter or a computer.

☞ The longest continuous piano piece ever published is four hours, twelve minutes, and ten seconds long. It's called The Well-Tuned Piano.

Which instrument is played everywhere?

The drum. All over the world, people bang out rhythms on different kinds of drums. They tap, slap, and hit drums to beat out the rhythms of their music. Drums sound different notes depending on how tight or loose the drumskin is.

12

Play that tune!
Caribbean musicians play tunes on empty steel oil drums. The top is hammered into bumps of different sizes. Each bump sounds different when it is hit, so the drummer can play tunes.

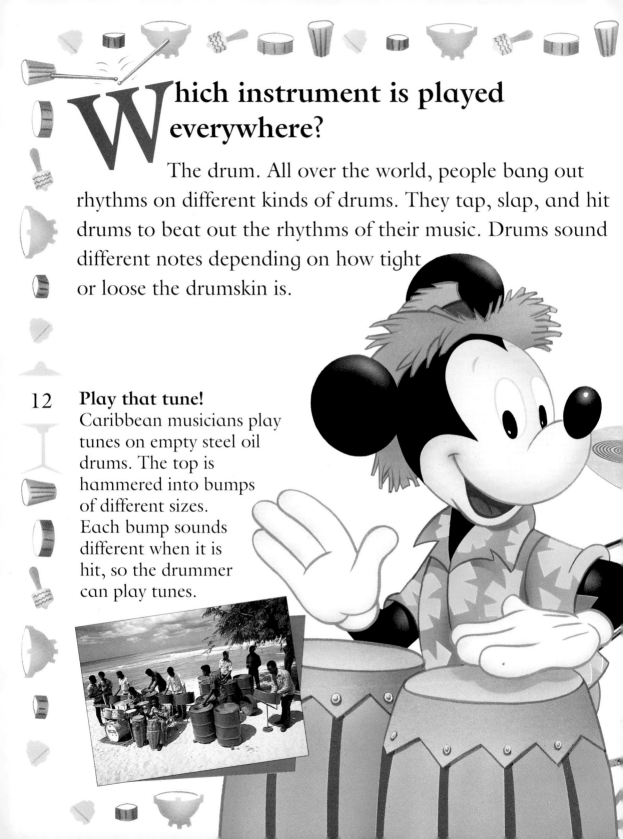

Dazzling drum facts

👉 The bigger the drum, the lower the note it sounds. The big bass drum makes a low, deep, "thunking" sound.

👉 You can make a drum kit of your own from cookie tins, cartons, and plastic containers. But you may have to go practice in the park!

Ta da!
Who's at the door?
A man with a drum.
Tell him to beat it!

How did people long ago learn new songs?

Singers would wander around the countryside, going from castle to castle, from town to town, playing and singing the songs they knew. These wandering musicians were called minstrels. Other minstrels would hear the songs, learn them by heart, and set off on their own travels, spreading the tunes far and wide.

The latest hits

About a hundred years ago, people used to rush to the sheet music store to buy a written-down copy of the latest hit song. They would play the song at home on a piano or guitar.

Pop facts

 The song most often sung in English is "Happy Birthday to You." It was written by two Sunday school teachers from Kentucky who called it "Good Morning to All."

How many instruments are there in an orchestra?

An orchestra is made up of four families of instruments – string, woodwind, brass, and percussion. Full orchestras can range in size from about 80 people to hundreds of people. The conductor, who is the person in charge of the orchestra, waves a baton to keep all the musicians playing together.

16

Bright sounds
Brass instruments, like horns, trumpets, and trombones, are made of a metal called brass. They are played by blowing.

Piping sounds
Woodwind instruments, like flutes and clarinets, were once made of wood. Now they are often made of metal or plastic. They are also played by blowing.

Sweet sounds
String instruments are violins, violas, cellos, and double basses. They are plucked and bowed.

Keeping the beat
Percussion instruments are drums, cymbals, and anything you hit to make a sound.

17

All together now!

Not all the instruments play the same notes at the same time. Some instruments play the high notes, while others sound low and deep. And different instruments play different tunes that sound good together.

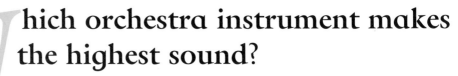

Which orchestra instrument makes the highest sound?

The piccolo makes just about the highest sound. A piccolo is a tiny little flute with a high, piercing sound. A big brass tuba makes a very, very low sound. If you could see sound waves, a high sound would look like lots of fast-moving wiggles – a low sound would look like a slow, lazy wave.

Hitting the high notes

Some animals can hear very high sounds. Certain dog whistles, for instance, make a sound so high we can't hear it, but dogs can. Woof woof!

Oompah pah! Mickey's playing a sousaphone. It's a kind of tuba developed by John Sousa, who is famous for composing march music.

Come on home, Bessie! Some alpenhorns are more than 12 feet long. They aren't actually musical instruments; they were made for Swiss farmers to call their cattle home.

What is the largest musical instrument?

The pipe organ. An organ is made of pipes of different sizes. Little pipes make the high notes. They can be just an inch tall. The pipes that make the deep sounds can be as tall as a house. When the player presses the keys on the keyboard, a flap opens inside the organ which allows air to pass through certain pipes – and that is where the sound comes from.

A bag of wind

Bagpipes are one of the oldest instruments of all. Roman soldiers used them in their military bands over 2,000 years ago. Wind from the bag gets forced through the pipes to make a droning sound – well, some people like it!

Outrageous organ facts

 The biggest (and loudest) organ ever made is in Atlantic City, New Jersey. It has twelve keyboards and 33,112 pipes. It could make as much noise as 25 brass bands!

Useful composers
What did the musician take to the supermarket?
A Chopin Liszt!

How many instruments can one person play at once?

It takes a lot of skill and practice, but some people can manage a guitar, a harmonica and a kazoo on a special neck harness – along with a couple of drums and some jangling rattles on their legs, cymbals on their elbows, and maybe some bells on their hat!

Bet you didn't know that...

A composer named Leopold Mozart wrote a piece of music that uses musical toys such as rattles, whistles, and humming tops.

Big mouth!
Some people can play
more than one wind
instrument at once.

Marching bands
Musicians who play in
marching bands have to
hold their instruments, play
them and march in step at
the same time – so don't
expect to see a piano
marching by!

23

How does a piano make music?

Little hammers hit the strings inside! When you press on a key, a little felt-covered hammer hits one of the strings. The string vibrates and makes a sound. The piano can be played loud or soft depending on how hard you hit the keys.

24

Play it again, kids!

The first pianos had strings on a horizontal frame. The upright piano was made so people could fit this popular instrument through their front doors.

Strings attached

The harp is also a string instrument. Its strings are plucked.

Piano pieces

In Victorian England, people often covered up the legs of their pianos because they thought pianos shouldn't show their legs!

Awesome sound
Piano Tuner: I've come to tune your piano.
Boy: But I didn't send for you.
Piano Tuner: No, but your neighbors did!

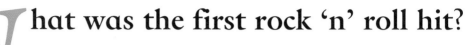What was the first rock 'n' roll hit?

"Rock Around the Clock," which was recorded by Bill Haley and the Comets in 1954. Rock 'n' roll music is happy, upbeat music. It was new because it was music played by young people for young people, and it was written for electric guitars and small bands instead of pianos and big orchestras.

The King
Elvis Presley is often called the king of rock 'n' roll. He helped to make rock music VERY popular. He had his first big hit in 1956 with the song "Heartbreak Hotel."

Powerful sounds

☞ The electric guitar works by turning the vibrations of the strings into powerful electric signals. It can make wild and wonderful sounds, but only when it's plugged in!

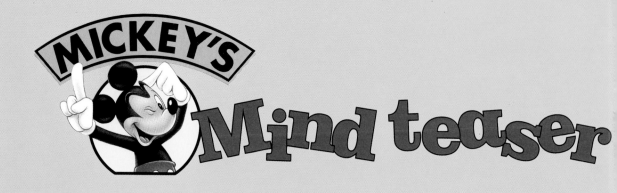

MICKEY'S Mind teaser

Of the four instruments below – which ones are hit and which ones are plucked?